The Road to
San Jacinto:
Texas Gains Independence

Edited by Mary Dodson Wade

Discovery Enterprises, Ltd.
Carlisle, Massachusetts

© Discovery Enterprises, Ltd., Carlisle, MA: 1997

ISBN 1-878668-62-5 paperback edition
Library of Congress Catalog Card Number 96-84754

10 9 8 7 6 5 4 3 2 1

Printed in the United States of America

Subject Reference Guide:

The Road to San Jacinto: Texas Gains Independence
edited by Mary Dodson Wade

Texas History

Photos/Illustrations:

Front cover: Detail from William H. Huddle, *The Surrender of Santa Anna*, 1886, oil painting, original in The State Capitol, Austin. Courtesy of The Texas State Library, Archives Division, Austin.

Map on page 4 by Bill Hoffman.

Page 14: The San Jacinto Museum of History, Houston, Texas and The Center for American History, The University of Texas at Austin.

All other illustrations: The San Jacinto Museum of History, Houston, Texas.

Acknowledgments

The editor and publisher are extremely grateful to
Brian Butcher, Assistant Director of Museum Operations,
The San Jacinto Museum of History, for his very substantial help.
A number of others also helped. Although limited space
prevents us from naming them individually, we thank them all.

Table of Contents

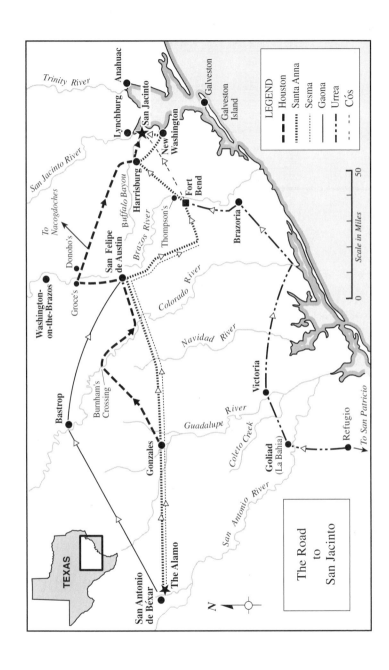

The Road
to
San Jacinto

LEGEND
Houston
Santa Anna
Sesma
Gaona
Urrea
Cós

Scale in Miles
0 50

N

TEXAS

Trinity River
Anahuac
Lynchburg
San Jacinto
New Washington
Galveston
Galveston Island
San Jacinto River
To Nacogdoches
Harrisburg
Buffalo Bayou
Donoho's
San Felipe de Austin
Fort Bend
Brazos River
Thompson's
Brazoria
Washington-on-the-Brazos
Groce's
Colorado River
Bastrop
Navidad River
Burnham's Crossing
Victoria
Guadalupe River
Gonzales
Coleto Creek
Refugio
To San Patricio
San Antonio de Béxar
The Alamo
San Antonio River
Goliad (La Bahía)

Introduction

by
Mary Dodson Wade

Widow Margaret McCormick's land lay along Buffalo Bayou at the point where it joins the San Jacinto River. Middle-aged and illiterate, she made a good living in the 1830s raising cattle with the help of her two sons. With the sudden approach of the Mexican army in the spring of 1836, Peggy left cattle in the field and retreated eastward to safety. While she was gone, Sam Houston's rag-tag Texas army defeated Mexican forces under Antonio López de Santa Anna. An eighteen-minute battle fought on her land on April 21, 1836, changed the political face of North America.

Early engagements between the two adversaries had not indicated such a dramatic end to their confrontation. The Texans began their bid to obtain statehood within the Mexican nation in the early 1830s and continued it for a number of years until, in time, they came to see it as futile. When they declared independence on March 2, 1836, the Mexican dictator moved swiftly to put down the revolt. Already in San Antonio with a large army to avenge the Texans' expulsion of Mexican troops the previous December, Santa Anna issued orders to spare no one who bore arms against Mexico.

On March 6, 1836, defenders of the Alamo died to a man, and Santa Anna began an eastward sweep to crush any remaining resistance. Houston's army, arriving at Gonzales nearly a week later, found reports of the tragedy from Juan Seguín's scouts. Erastus "Deaf" Smith, whom Houston sent for confirmation, returned with survivors Susanna Dickinson, her daughter Angelina, and William Travis's slave named Joe. At midnight on March 13, Houston's army and the grieving relatives of men who died at the Alamo abandoned Gonzales.

Santa Anna and his second in command, General Vicente Filisola, sent three armies in pursuit. General Antonio Gaona took a northern route toward Nacogdoches. General José Urrea was on a southern track. General Joaquín Ramírez y Sesma followed Houston, generally on a middle course.

Retreating toward Anglo settlements, Houston gained volunteers daily, but his force was no match for the one advancing on him. From the Navidad River on March 15, he sent word to the Texas officials at Washington-on-the-Brazos that the army would fall back to the Colorado.

The volunteers in the army, untrained but ready to fight, grumbled about the retreat. On the nineteenth, the Texas army, six hundred strong, crossed to the east bank of the Colorado. Almost immediately, Ramírez y Sesma's forces reached the river but had no way to cross. For a week the two armies eyed each other from opposite banks, but no battle occurred.

Houston had sent word to Colonel James Walker Fannin to abandon Goliad and retreat to Victoria, but the colonel delayed, reluctant to abandon the fortifications he had made. When Fannin's men began to move on the nineteenth, Urrea's forces caught them in an open area near Coleto Creek. After an exhausting afternoon of battle and a cold night without food or water, Fannin surrendered, and the men returned to Goliad as prisoners. A week later, they were marched out under guard, with doctors and interpreters left behind. The Texans assumed they were to be released, but the orders were to shoot them. About thirty managed to escape by jumping into the river and swimming to safety, but some three hundred fifty Texans were executed that Palm Sunday.

As soon as Houston learned of Fannin's surrender, he ordered another retreat. In an extraordinary march his forces reached the Brazos at San Felipe de Austin on March 27, the day Fannin and his men were killed. The retreat did nothing to inspire confidence among the troops. Continuous rain fell. Cold, wet, and disheartened, many soldiers grew disgusted with a commander who refused to stand and fight. The ranks, which had swelled to fourteen hundred with American volunteers, thinned as men went home to see about their families.

Moving along with the army were panic-stricken colonists fleeing in what is called the Runaway Scrape. They abandoned livestock and left uneaten meals as they headed for safety in Louisiana. Rain dogged their every step. Women, children, slaves, and baggage piled up at rivers, waiting days to cross.

Houston stayed in San Felipe only one day. Now at the head of the only Texas force left, he turned north, away from the enemy, and encountered bitter criticism not only from the soldiers. Texas's provisional president, David G. Burnet, sent a scathing letter from Harrisburg. "The enemy are laughing you to scorn.…You must retreat no farther." But Houston refused to seek or take advice. Writing to his personal friend, Secretary of War Thomas Rusk, he said, "I consulted none. I held no council of war. If I err, the blame is mine."

Two militia leaders, Mosely Baker and Wily Martin, openly refused to follow Houston upriver. Baker was left to prevent Mexican troops from crossing the Brazos at San Felipe, while Martin was ordered downriver thirty miles to Fort Bend to prevent a crossing there.

Muddy conditions turned the fifteen-mile trip up the Brazos into a three-day ordeal. During the next week and a half, camped at Groce's plantation, Houston set up commands and drilled soldiers. An outbreak of measles made bad conditions worse. The Brazos was running bank to bank, and the steamer *Yellow-Stone*, loading cotton at Groce's landing, was pressed into service to move troops across.

In the meantime, Santa Anna joined Ramírez y Sesma at the Colorado on April 4. Three days later, at burned-out San Felipe on the Brazos, a captured Texan told them that Houston was nearby, planning to escape to the United States. Checked by Baker's men, Ramírez y Sesma moved downstream to Fort Bend where his larger numbers forced Martin to retire. Mexican troops began to cross the Brazos.

Ignoring Houston's small force, Santa Anna turned to catch another prize: Texas officials at Harrisburg. To speed travel, he left Fort Bend on April 14 with seven hundred troops after ordering Ramírez y

Sesma to wait there for reinforcements.

By April 13, Houston had all his troops across the Brazos. The arrival of two cannons from Cincinnati, nicknamed the "Twin Sisters," buoyed spirits, but the order to march in the direction of Donoho's farm caused concern among soldiers who wanted to fight. They knew that about twelve miles beyond Donoho's, the road split; one branch led to Harrisburg and the enemy and the other, to Nacogdoches and the United States.

Pulling the cannons along the muddy roads were oxen belonging to Mrs. Pamela Mann, who was headed to Nacogdoches. Houston had assured her his troops were going in the same direction but had issued no orders on the matter.

As soldiers reached the fork on the 16th, a shout went up, "To the right, to the right." All formations turned south toward Harrisburg. As the troops headed south, Mrs. Mann rode up in a fury. Calling Houston a liar, she cut her oxen free, and the cannons sank in the mud. Houston dismounted and helped pull them out. The wagonmaster followed Mrs. Mann to protest but returned empty-handed.

On the previous day, Santa Anna had reached Harrisburg where he found the town deserted except for three printers putting out a newspaper. From them he learned that members of the government had embarked by steamer for New Washington. Houston, they said, was on his way to the United States by way of Lynch's Ferry, a few miles to the east. Santa Anna ordered the printing press dumped into Buffalo Bayou, torched Harrisburg, and sent General Juan Nepomuceno Almonte down the coast with a small force in hopes of capturing President Burnet and his cabinet. Burnet was pulling away from shore in a boat as the Mexicans arrived, but Almonte refused to fire on them because Mrs. Burnet was aboard. The party escaped to Galveston.

Santa Anna arrived at New Washington, and while he was inspecting supplies there on the eighteenth, Houston was bringing his troops into burned-out Harrisburg. Soon "Deaf" Smith and Henry Karnes arrived with a captured Mexican courier. From the letters he was carrying Houston learned that Santa Anna was separated from the main army, with troops equal in number to his own — a perfect opportunity for battle. Crucial as this information was, it was the saddlebags themselves that rallied Houston's soldiers to a fighting pitch. They were booty taken at the Alamo and bore the name of William Barret Travis.

Leaving seventy-five soldiers to guard baggage and care for ill soldiers, Houston pushed the rest of his troops eastward to cut off Santa Anna. The Texan army crossed Buffalo Bayou and did not halt for rest until midnight. At six in the morning — the twentieth — their breakfast was interrupted when the Mexican army was sighted returning from New Washington. The Texans raced to the oak grove on the neck of land where Buffalo Bayou joins the San Jacinto River and later that morning feasted on captured provisions Santa Anna had sent upriver.

The two armies faced each other across Peggy McCormick's field. A skirmish occurred, but no real damage was done. The Mexican army pitched camp on the edge of the bayou and made a barricade of saddles, baggage, and brush.

Early on the twenty-first, General Martín Perfecto de Cós, Santa Anna's brother-in-law, arrived with about 540 dead-tired reinforcements. They had crossed Vince's Bridge shortly before "Deaf" Smith's crew destroyed the structure.

As the day wore on without orders, the Texans became convinced that there would be no fight. Santa Anna, believing the same, put his camp at ease and stretched out to sleep under a tree. Mexican soldiers busied themselves with cooking, repairing equipment, and taking their horses to water.

Then, shortly after three o'clock in the afternoon, Houston formed up a long, double line of soldiers with the cavalry on the right. Juan Seguín's Tejanos wore cardboard in their hatbands to distinguish them as allies. Raising his sword, the Texas commander signaled his troops forward. Moving silently across nearly a mile of open prairie, their advance hidden by a small rise of ground, the Texans were almost on the Mexican line when they struck up the bawdy song, "Will You Come to the Bower I Have Shaded for You?"

The Mexican bugler sounded the alarm at 4:30 P.M., and pandemonium broke loose. The first shot from the "Twin Sisters" blew a hole in the Mexican line. Texas soldiers shouting, "Remember the Alamo!" and, "Remember Goliad!" overran their enemy's position. Unable to reload, they used any weapon at hand. Mexican soldiers dived into the river only to be picked off as they swam. In the madness that followed, the Texans pursued the Mexicans into the water. Dead horses and human bodies formed a bridge.

Houston, riding at the front, was wounded when his horse Saracen went down. He was on his third horse before the day was over.

The battle lasted less than twenty minutes, but the killing went on until dark. Officers called for formation, but the soldiers were out of control. Houston shouted, "Gentlemen! I can win wars with you, but damn your manners." No one listened.

According to Houston's report, two of his 783 men were killed and six were mortally wounded, while 630—undoubtedly an over-estimate—of the Mexican soldiers were killed. Almonte had managed to get some order among a number of soldiers around him, and they surrendered. In all, Houston writes—again probably exaggerating somewhat—730 Mexicans were captured. But the prize was missing. Santa Anna was nowhere to be found.

The dictator and his personal secretary, Ramón Martínez Caro, fled on horseback toward Harrisburg only to reach the demolished bridge. Santa Anna abandoned Caro and fled into the brush. During the night, as patrols searched the surrounding area, he made his way to a farm and found old clothing. The shirt went on over his fine linen one with diamond studs, but he kept on the red slippers in which he had escaped.

The next day when a patrol brought him into camp not knowing who he was, Mexican soldiers began to shout, "El Presidente!" Unable to conceal his identity, Santa Anna asked to be taken to Houston.

The Texas commander was propped against a tree because of

his shattered ankle. There were angry calls to execute the Mexican leader, but Houston motioned for him to sit on a nearby box. With Moses Austin Bryan, Lorenzo de Zavala, Jr., and Almonte acting as interpreters, Santa Anna complimented Houston on capturing "The Napoleon of the West." Unimpressed, Houston spoke of the slaughter at Goliad. He waved aside Santa Anna's excuse that he was following government orders, pointing out that Santa Anna *was* the government. Bravado gone, the dictator agreed to send Filisola orders to retreat with the remaining soldiers.

Santa Anna's silk tent was set up next to where Houston lay on a mattress. For a week the wounded Texas commander wrote reports. When Filisola received Santa Anna's orders, it astonished everyone, including the Mexican officers, that he followed them. The Mexican force still in Texas was substantially larger than the Texan army, but it turned and retreated.

On the battlefield the bodies of Mexican soldiers lay where they had fallen. Lorenzo de Zavala, whose house across the river had served the Texans as a hospital, found the body of his friend, General Manuel Fernandez Castrillón, and took it to his house for burial.

When President Burnet arrived to take charge of Santa Anna, his dislike for Houston made him refuse the wounded commander permission to board the *Yellow-Stone* to go for treatment. The captain of the ship, however, refused to leave without the Hero of San Jacinto.

Peggy McCormick returned home to find that her cattle had been devoured by both friend and foe. Worse than that, hundreds of slain Mexican soldiers lay in her field. Protests did not get them moved, and months later she and her sons buried the bleached bones. To Mrs. McCormick the battle was a personal disaster, but for Texans at large it changed everything. Texas was free.

Disaster at Goliad

John Crittenden Duval, born in Kentucky, caught "Texas Fever" at age nineteen. Educated for his time, he arrived in the fall of 1835, joining Fannin at Goliad but escaping the massacre although his brother Burr did not.

The document Fannin signed in surrendering to Urrea indicated that the surrender was "at discretion," that is, unconditional. By contrast, Fannin's troops who survived the subsequent massacre thought that their commander had managed to negotiate more favorable terms. Duval was adamant in his belief that Fannin had not surrendered "at discretion."

Source: J. C. Duval, *Early Times in Texas* (Austin: H. P. N. Gammel & Co., 1892; reprint, Austin: The Steck Company, 1935), pp. 48-59.

Our loss in the Coletto fight was ten killed and about seventy wounded (Col. Fannin among the latter), and most of them badly, owing to the size of the balls thrown by the Mexican escopetas [muskets], and the shotguns of the Indians. The number of our casualties was extremely small considering the force of the enemy, and the duration of the fight, which began about three o'clock and lasted till nearly sunset....

I can never forget how slowly the hours of that dismal night passed by. The distressing cries of our wounded men begging for water when there was not a drop to give them, were continually ringing in my ears....

Daylight at last appeared, and before the sun had risen we saw that the Mexican forces were all in motion, and evidently preparing to make another attack upon us....

[Later] the Mexicans again made a show of attacking us, but just as we were expecting them to charge, Gen. Urrea himself rode out in front of his lines accompanied by several of his officers and the soldier with the "white flag.["] Col. Fannin and Major Wallace went out to meet them, and the terms of capitulation were finally agreed upon, the most important of which was, that we should be held as prisoners of war until exchanged, or liberated on our parole of honor not to engage in the war again — at the option o[f] the Mexican commander in chief....

...[I]t was reduced to writing, and an English translation given to Col. Fannin which was read to our men. I am thus particular in stating what I know to be the facts in regard to this capitulation, because I have seen it stated that Gen. Santa Anna always asserted there was no capitulation, and that Col. Fannin surrendered at discretion to Gen. Urrea. This assertion I have no doubt was made to justify as far as possible his order for the cold blooded murder of disarmed prisoners....

A day or so after our return as prisoners to Goliad...those who survived the engagement they had with the Mexicans, near Refugio, were brought in and confined with us....

One day an officer who was passing, asked me some question in Spanish, and when I answered him in Spanish he took a seat by me. ...He expressed much astonishment at the correctness of my pronunciation, and asked where I had learned to speak Spanish, saying he was sure I had not learnt the language among the Mexicans. I told him I had studied Spanish under a teacher of modern languages at a Catholic institution in Kentucky....

On the morning of the 27th of March, a Mexican officer came....He told us we were to be liberated on "parole," and that arrangements had been made to send us to New Orleans on board of vessels then at Copano....When all was ready we were formed into three divisions and marched out under a strong guard. As we passed by some Mexican women who were standing near the main entrance to the fort, I heard them say "pobrecitos" (poor fellows), but the incident at the time made but little impression on my mind.

One of our divisions was taken down the road leading to the lower ford of the river, one upon the road to San Patricio, and the division to which my company was attached, along the road leading to San

Andrew Jackson Houston, The March to the Massacre, date unknown, oil painting. Andrew Jackson Houston was Sam and Margaret Houston's son, one of their many children.

Antonio. A strong guard accompanied us, marching in double files on both sides of our column. It occurred to me that this division of our men into three squads, and marching us off in three directions, was rather a singular maneuver, but still I had no suspicion of the foul play intended us. When about half a mile above town, a halt was made and the guard on the side next the river filed around to the opposite side. Hardly had this maneuver been executed, when I heard a heavy firing of musketry in the directions taken by the other two divisions. Some one near me exclaimed "Boys! they are going to shoot us!" and at the same instant I heard the clicking of musket locks all along the Mexican line. I turned to look, and as I did so, the Mexicans fired upon us, killing probably one hundred out of the one hundred and fifty men in the division. We were in double file and I was in the rear rank. The man in front of me was shot dead, and in falling he knocked me down. I did not get up for a moment, and when I rose to my feet, I found that the whole Mexican line had charged over me, and were in hot pursuit of those who had not been shot and who were fleeing towards the river about five hundred yards distant. I followed on after them, for I knew that escape in any other direction (all open prairie) would be impossible, and I had nearly reached the river before it became necessary to make my way through the Mexican line ahead. As I did so, one of the soldiers charged upon me with his bayonet (his gun I suppose being empty). As he drew his musket back to make a lunge at me, one of our men coming from another direction, ran between us, and the bayonet was driven through his body....I hastened to the bank of the river and plunged in. The river at that point was deep and swift, but not wide, and being a good swimmer, I soon gained the opposite bank, untouched by any of the bullets that were pattering in the water around my head....The bank on that side was so steep I found it was impossible to climb it, and I continued to swim down the river until I came to where a grape vine hung from the bough of a leaning tree nearly to the surface of the water. This I caught hold of and was climbing up it hand over hand, sailor fashion, when a Mexican on

15

the opposite bank fired at me with his escopeta, and with so true an aim, that he cut the vine in two just above my head, and down I came into the water again. I then swam on about a hundred yards further, when I came to a place where the bank was not quite so steep, and with some difficulty I managed to clamber up....

The river on the north side was bordered by timber several hundred yards in width, through which I quickly passed....

...I saw a young man by the name of Holliday, one of my own messmates....I called to him as loudly as I dared....

A few moments afterwards we were joined by a young man by the name of Brown, from Georgia....

...[W]e came to the conclusion that in all probability we were the only survivors of the hundreds who had that morning been led out to slaughter; although in fact as we subsequently learned, twenty-five or thirty of our men eventually reached the settlements on the Brazos. Drs. Shackleford and Barnard, our surgeons, were saved from the massacre to attend upon Mexicans wounded in the fight on the Coletto....Our own wounded men...were carried out into the open square of the fort, and there cruelly butchered by the guard....

Col. Fannin, who was confined to his quarters by a wound he had received at the fight on the Coletto, soon after the massacre of his men, was notified to prepare for immediate execution. He merely [o]bserved that he was ready then, as he had no desire to live after the cold-blooded, cowardly murder of his men. He was thereupon taken out to the square by a guard, where he was seated on a bench, and his eyes blindfolded. A moment before the order to "fire" was given, I was told (though I cannot vouch for the truth of the statement) he drew a fine gold watch from his pocket, and handing it to the officer in command of the guard, requested him as a last favor to order his men to shoot him in the breast and not in the head. The officer took the watch, and immediately ordered the guard to fire at his head. Col. Fannin fell dead and his body was thrown into one of the ravines near the fort. Thus died as brave a son of Georgia as ever came from that noble old State.

Flight across Texas

Dilue Rose's family lived near Fort Bend. Shortly before she became eleven, they joined other settlers fleeing eastward in the direction of the United States and safety. Later in life, as Mrs. Harris, she added her own comments to those her father, Dr. Pleasant W. Rose, a physician, had kept in a journal.

Source: Dilue Harris, "The Reminiscences of Mrs. Dilue Harris. II.," *The Quarterly of the Texas State Historical Association* 4, no. 3 (January, 1901), pp. 161-68.

By the 20th of February the people of San Patricio and other western settlements were fleeing for their lives. Every family in our neighborhood was preparing to go to the United States. Wagons and other vehicles were scarce.…

…On the 12th of March came the news of the fall of the Alamo. A courier brought a dispatch from General Houston for the people to leave. Colonel Travis and the men under his command had been slaughtered, the Texas army was retreating, and President Burnet's cabinet had gone to Harrisburg.

Then began the horrors of the "Runaway Scrape." We left home at sunset, hauling clothes, bedding, and provisions on the sleigh with one yoke of oxen. Mother and I were walking, she with an infant in her arms. Brother drove the oxen, and my two little sisters rode in the sleigh. We were going ten miles to where we could be transferred to Mr. Bundick's cart. Father was helping with the cattle, but he joined us after dark and brought a horse and saddle for brother. He sent him to help Mr. Stafford with the cattle. He was to go a different road with them and ford the San Jacinto. Mother and I then rode father's horse.…

It was ten o'clock at night when we got to Mrs. Roark's. We shifted our things into the cart of Mr. Bundick, who was waiting for us, and tried to rest till morning. Sister and I had been weeping all day about Colonel Travis. When we started from home we got the little books he had given us and would have taken them with us, but mother said it was best to leave them.

Early next morning we were on the move, mother with her four children in the cart, and Mr. Bundick and his wife and negro woman on horseback. He had been in bad health for some time and had just got home from visiting his mother, who lived in Louisiana. He brought with him two slaves, the woman already mentioned and a man who was driving the cart; and, as Mr. Bundick had no children, we were as comfortable as could have been expected....

...Next day we crossed Vince's Bridge and arrived at the San Jacinto in the night. There were fully five thousand people at the ferry. The planters from Brazoria and Columbia with their slaves were crossing. We waited three days before we crossed. Our party consisted of five white families: father's, Mr. Dyer's, Mr. Bell's, Mr. Neal's, and Mr. Bundick's. Father and Mr. Bundick were the only white men in the party, the others being in the army. There were twenty or thirty negroes from Stafford's plantation. They had a large wagon with five yoke of oxen, and horses, and mules, and they were in charge of an old negro man called Uncle Ned. Altogether, black and white, there were about fifty of us. Every one was trying to cross first, and it was almost a riot.

We got over the third day, and after travelling a few miles came to a big prairie. It was about twelve miles further to the next timber and water, and some of our party wanted to camp; but others said that the Trinity river was rising, and if we delayed we might not get across. So we hurried on....

Our hardships began at the Trinity. The river was rising and there was a struggle to see who should cross first. Measles, sore eyes, whooping cough, and every other disease that man, woman, or child is heir to, broke out among us. Our party now consisted of the five white families I first mentioned, and Mr. Adam Stafford's negroes. We had separated from Mrs. M—. and other friends at Vince's bridge. The horrors of crossing the Trinity are beyond my power to describe.

One of my little sisters was very sick, and the ferryman said that those families that had sick children should cross first. When our party got to the boat the water broke over the banks above where we were and ran around us. We were several hours surrounded by water. Our family was the last to get to the boat. We left more than five hundred people on the...west bank. Drift wood covered the water as far as we could see. The sick child was in convulsions. It required eight men to manage the boat.

When we landed the lowlands were under water, and everybody was rushing for the prairie. Father had a good horse, and Mrs. Dyer let mother have her horse and saddle. Father carried the sick child, and sister and I rode behind mother. She carried father's gun and the little babe. All we carried with us was what clothes we were wearing at the time. The night was very dark. We crossed a bridge that was under water. As soon as we crossed, a man with a cart and oxen drove on the bridge, and it broke down, drowing the oxen. That prevented the people from crossing, as the bridge was over a slough that looked like a river.

Father and mother hurried on, and we got to the prairie and found a great many families camped there. A Mrs. Foster invited mother to her camp, and furnished us with supper, a bed, and dry clothes.

The other families stayed all night in the bottom without fire or anything to eat, and the water up in the carts. The men drove the horses and oxen to the prairies, and the women, sick children, and negroes were left in the bottom. The old negro man, Uncle Ned, was left in charge. He put the white women and children in his wagon. It was large and had a canvas cover. The negro women and their children he put in the carts. Then he guarded the whole party until morning.

It was impossible for the men to return to their families. They spent the night making a raft by torch light. As the camps were near a grove of pine timber, there was no trouble about lights. It was a night of terror. Father and the men worked some distance from the camp cutting down timber to make the raft. It had to be put together in the water. We were in great anxiety about the people that were left in the bottom; we didn't know but they would be drowned, or killed by panthers, alligators, or bears.

As soon as it was daylight the men went to the relief of their families and found them cold, wet, and hungry. Many of the families that were water bound I didn't know; but there were among them Mrs. Bell's three children, and Mrs. Dyer and her sister, Mrs. Neal, with five children....It was very dangerous crossing the slough. The men would bring one woman and her children on the raft out of deep water, and men on horseback would meet them. It took all day to get the party out to the prairies. The men had to carry cooked provisions to them.

The second day they brought out the bedding and clothes. Everything was soaked with water. They had to take the wagon and carts apart....It took four days to get everything out of the water.

The man whose oxen were drowned sold his cart to father for ten dollars. He said that he had seen enough of Mexico and would go back to old Ireland.

It had been five days since we crossed the Trinity, and we had heard no news from the army. The town of Liberty was three miles from where we camped. The people there had not left their homes, and they gave us all the help in their power. My little sister that had been sick died and was buried in the cemetery at Liberty. After resting a few days our party continued their journey, but we remained in the town. Mother was not able to travel; she had nursed an infant and the sick child until she was compelled to rest.

A few days after our friends had gone a man crossed the Trinity in a skiff bringing bad news. The Mexican army had crossed the Brazos and was between the Texas army and Harrisburg. Fannin and his men were massacred. President Burnet and his cabinet had left Harrisburg and gone to Washington on the bay and were going to Galveston Island. The people at Liberty had left. There were many families west of the Trinity, among them our nearest neighbors, Mrs. Roark and Mrs. M—....

We had been at Liberty three weeks. A Mr. Martin let father use his house....One Thursday evening all of a sudden we heard a sound like distant thunder. When it was repeated father said it was cannon, and that the Texans and Mexicans were fighting. He had been through the war of 1812, and knew it was a battle. The cannonading lasted only a few minutes, and father said that the Texans must have been defeated, or the cannon would not have ceased firing so quickly. We left Liberty in half an hour. The reports of the cannon were so distant that father was under the impression that the fighting was near the Trinity. The river was ten miles wide at Liberty.

We travelled nearly all night, sister and I on horseback and mother in the cart. Father had two yoke of oxen now. One yoke belonged to Adam Stafford and had strayed and father found them. The extra yoke was a great help as the roads were very boggy. We rested a few hours to let the stock feed. Mr. Bright and two families were with us. We were as wretched as we could be; for we had been five weeks from home, and there was not much prospect of our ever returning. We had not heard a word from brother or the other boys that were driving the cattle. Mother was sick, and we had buried our dear little sister at Liberty.

We continued our journey through mud and water and when we camped in the evening fifty or sixty young men came by who were going to join General Houston. One of them was Harvey Stafford, our neighbor, who was returning from the United States with volunteers. Father told them there had been fighting, and he informed them that they could not cross the Trinity at Liberty. They brought some good news from our friends. Mr. Stafford had met his sisters, Mrs. Dyer, and Mrs. Neal. He said there had been a great deal of sickness, but no deaths. He said also that General Gaines of the United States army was at the Neches with a regiment of soldiers to keep the Indians in subjection, but didn't prevent the people from crossing with their slaves. General Gaines said the boundary line between the United States and Mexico was the Neches.

The young men went a short distance from us and camped. Then we heard some one calling in the direction of Liberty. We could see a man on horseback waving his hat; and, as we knew there was no one left at Liberty, we thought the Mexican army had crossed the Trinity. The young men came with their guns, and when the rider got near enough for us to understand what he said, it was "Turn back! The Texas army has whipped the Mexican army and the Mexican army are prisoners. No danger! No danger! Turn back!" When he got to the camp he could scarcely speak he was so excited and out of breath. When the young men began to understand the glorious news they wanted to fire a salute, but father made them stop. He told them to save their ammunition, for they might need it.

Father asked the man for an explanation, and he showed a despatch from General Houston giving an account of the battle and saying it would be safe for the people to return to their homes. The courier had crossed the Trinity River in a canoe, swimming his horse with the help of two men. He had left the battle field the next day after the fighting. He said that General Houston was wounded, and that General Santa Anna had not been captured.

In the Words of Some Participants

Hunter had been in Texas since 1822 and was twenty-two when he helped drive Cós out of San Antonio. He was on baggage detail in Harrisburg and missed the battle of San Jacinto, but he gives a lively account of the events leading to it, recording Sam Houston's encounters with two strong-willed women.

Source: Robert Hancock Hunter, *The Narrative of Robert Hancock Hunter*, with an introduction by William D. Wittliff (Austin: The Encino Press, 1966), pp. 9-18.

...A Currer came to our place on the Brassos in Fort Bend Co. He shoed his dispach, stating that Colonel Travis wanted men to defend the Alamo. Brother John, Robert Mc Anella and his brother Pleasant Mc Anella, & Merdeth Tunget and myself, was on the top the ginn house nailing on shingles. Father said Well Boys who of you is going to Travis. I said, I am one, & the balance all said I with you....We got our horses & extry suit of clothes & some grub & guns, & left for camp....

[On the way, they learned the fate of the Alamo and were ordered to head for a rendezvous with Houston's troops. Ed.]

That same morning two women with 5 children with bundles of clothing on there heads came up. The Capt ast them, which way are you going. We are trying to git a way from the Mexicans....[W]e left our supper on the table, & we took what little clothing we could carry & our children & left....Capt told Leuitenant McCallister to throw them boxes [of tobacco] out of the waggon & give room for those women & children. Hell Capt that tobacco was given to the company....[The Captain] took the ax & chopt the boxes to peaces, & throw it out on the ground & cald his men to come & git there tabacco....A bout this time General Houstons army come a long, & the Capt haled them, Boys dont you want some tobacco. They holloid out yes. Here help yourselves, & they took all the tobacco. That gave room for the women & children, so we got them all a bord. General Houston Army past on, & we fell in rear gard....

[In time they reached the Brazos, crossed it, and moved on. Ed.]

Detail from lithograph of the Yellow-Stone *by Judith-Ann Saks, date unknown*

...Mrs Mann, with her two waggons & teams was at Mr Groces. General Houston, got a yoke of oxen from Mrs Mann to help the cannon a long. There had bin a greatdel of rain & roads was very bad. Mrs Mann said to general Houston, general, if you are going on the Nacogdoches road you can have my oxen, but if you go the other to Harrisburg you cant have them, for I want them myself. Houston said well I am going the Nacogdoches road but he did not say how far he would go on it. Any how the oxen come, & we started. About 6 miles on the road they forked, & the Harrisburg road turned to the right, all most rightagle down east & we got a bout 10 or 12 miles down the road, and Mrs Mann over took us, out on the big prairie hog wallow & full of water, & a very hot day. She rode up to the general, & said, general you tole me a d-m lie, you said that was going on the Nacogdoches road. Sir I want my oxen. Well Mrs Mann we cant spare them. We cant git our cannon a long with out them. I dont care a d-m for your cannon, I want my oxen. She had a pare of holster pistols on her saddle pummel & a very large kinfe on her saddle. She turned a round to the oxen, & jumpt down with knife & cut the raw hide tug that the chane was tide with. The log chane hook was broke & it was tide with raw hide. No body said a word. She jumpt on her horse with whipin hand, & away she went in a lope with her oxen. Capt Rover [Rohrer] rode up to general Houston, & said general we cant git a long with out them oxen, the cannon is don boged down. Well we have to get a long the best we can, the general said. Well general I will go and bring them back. He said well. The Capt & a nother man started back for the oxen. The Capt got a hundred yeard or so, & the general rased up in his saddle, & hollowed, Capt Rover that woman will fite. The Capt said d-m her fiteing.

Houston jumpt down off his horse, & said come Boys, les git this cannon out of the mud. The mud was very near over his boot top. He put his shoulder to wheel, & 8 or 10 men more lade holt, & out she come, & on we went, & got down a bout 6 miles & campt at big mot of timber. A bout 9 or 10 oclock Capt Rover came in to camp, & he did not bring any oxen. The Boys hollowed out, hai Capt where is your oxen. She would not let me have them. How come your shirt tore so, & some of the Boys would say Mrs Mann tore it off him. What was that for. She wanted it for baby rags. Capt Rover was our waggon master.

[At Harrisburg Hunter was detailed to guard baggage and saw Cós's troops go by. Ed.]

...[A] bout 3 oclock in the evening, we hered a cannon fire, & a nother & a nother, three fired in sussesston, & stopt. About 2 minutes a nother fired, & the little twin sisters comenced. They popt like popcorn in a oven, & we could here the small arms very plane. Our prisiner [the captured courier] was the livelest fellow you ever seen while the cannon was firing. As soon as the big gun stopt, he

25

becum sulkey....It was a long time before he would talk, & he said that Sant Anna was whipt. How do you know. I dont here his guns....

[They were ordered to San Jacinto. Ed.]

The land that the Battle was fought on was the property of a widow woman Mrs Mc Cormac an irish woman. She came to camp to see General Houston. She wanted to know if he was a going to take them ded Mexicans off my leg [league, a measure of land]. They hant me the longes day I live. Houston told her no, he wanted Sant Anna to bury them, & he would not. Sant Anna said that it was not a Battle, that he cald it a massacre. Plage on him. What did he call the Alamo & Laberde [Goliad].

I seen Joel W Roberson & Silvester & Bostic bringing Sant Anna. They come by the Mexicans that was under gard. You could not have heard it thunder for the shouts from the prisoners, exclaming, vive, vive, vive, Sant Anna....General Houston ordered Sant Annas tent to be put up, & it was put in a bout 10 or 12 feet of Houstons tent. There was a large tree had bloed up by the roots, Houston tent was on one side of the log, & Sant Anna tent was on other of log. I & Merdith Tunget, stud by that log & garded Sant Anna....

...[A] bout 3 oclock in the evening the Mexicans baggae took fire. The baggae was all geathered up & piled all in one big pile, saddles, blankets, & all kind of clothing gun powder, araphahoes or pack saddles. Thare was small Boy looking at the pistols & snaping them, & the gard told him that he mite do some damage & to leave....The powder was scatered all over the ground. He was snaping the pistole in a mongst a pile of guns & set the hole pile a fire, & it was for a few minutes like a little battle....We were by the log that was bifore Sant Annas door when the firing comenced on the hill, & Sant Anna broke for the doore. We jurked up our guns, & presented them at his brest, & tolde him to halt. He got within 2 feet of the door, & stopt, & looked up strate in our eyes. We had our guns cocked on him....Every body jumpt for his gun, caws we thought that Col Ugawtechea & General Fillasola, & General Wool had come from Richmond & had attacked us....There is one thing a bout it, I know we were pritty badley scared.

26

Born in Tennessee in 1817, Winters moved to Texas with his family which settled in an area between the eastern and western branches of the San Jacinto River called the "Big Thicket." During the battle of San Jacinto, he served as an infantryman. He was nineteen.

Source: James Washington Winters, "An Account of the Battle of San Jacinto," *The Quarterly of the Texas State Historical Association* 6, no. 2 (October 1902), pp. 139-44.

[On the morning of] April 21, a council of war was held. Sometime before noon, Houston passed around among the men gathered at the campfires and asked us if we wanted to fight. We replied with a shout that we were most anxious to do so. Then Houston replied, "Very well, get your dinners and I will lead you into the fight, and if you whip them every one of you shall be a captain".

There had been so many "split ups" and differences that Houston preferred the opinions of the men themselves, feeling that before hazarding battle he must find whether they would enter the engagement with a will. For the men had marched so long without food or rest that, perhaps, they might not be physically prepared....

After dinner the men were ready for battle. I was in Sherman's division — left wing of attack — but under my own captain, Wm. Ware. Rusk started out with us, but turned and went with the artillery. When we ran over the ridge we lost sight of the rest. On beginning the battle, before we got in sight of the Mexicans, they began firing at us. They were lying down in the grass. We examined the places where many had been, and found as many as five ends of cartridges where each Mexican lay, so supposed that each man had fired at us as many as five times before we reached them. Their breastworks were composed of baggage, saddlebags, and brush, in all about four or five feet high. There was a gap eight or ten feet wide through which they fired the cannon. I saw Houston in the midst of the enemy's tents near the first regiment to the right. A Mexican officer tried to rally his men, but was soon dispatched by a rifle ball and fell from his horse. Our regiment passed beyond the Mexican's breastworks before we knew it, while our other two regiments came up in front of them, so then we did them up in short order. I never heard any halt ordered. We never halted. The battle was won in fifteen or eighteen minutes. The Mexican cavalry broke in disorder, while ours was hotly pursuing them. Houston had two horses killed from under him, and was on his third one before he passed the Mexican's works. We ran and fought fully two miles.

After the fight was ended Houston gave orders to form in line and march back to camp, but we paid no attention to him, as we were all shaking hands and rejoicing over the victory. Houston gave the order three times and still the men payed no attention to him. And he turned his horse around and said "Men, I can gain victories with you, but damn your manners," and rode on to camp.

Joel Robinson and Sylvester brought in Santa Anna. I was there when he was brought in; was digging the grave to bury our eight men. They passed by us and halted at our guard lines. The Mexican prisoners clapped their hands, and give other signs of joy, shouting, "Santa Anna, Santa Anna!" I dropped my tools and followed after them to Houston, who was lying on his cot at the camp near the bayou....

When Santa Anna was brought into camp some called out, "Shoot him, hang him!" General Houston ordered the men who made these threats taken away....The same day I found a dead Mexican who had silver in his belt — about ten dollars. The money had slipped out when he was shot. Orders were given that all money found be brought in to headquarters. I turned this in. Money so captured was distributed to the soldiers, the amount so distributed averaging almost $11 per man. Santa Anna's handsomely ornamented saddle was held up and the men voted that it should be given to General Houston. Other officers' saddles were sold. One brought as high as $300. *[Santa Anna's saddle was given to Houston, who gave it to his cousin, Robert Houston McEwen. Ed.]*

A native of Austria, Erath was in his early twenties when he arrived in Texas in 1835 with a college education and a command of languages. He fought under Houston at San Jacinto and cringed at the carnage of the battle. The following selection was developed from his memoirs which, in 1886, at the age of seventy-three, he dictated to his daughter Lucy who, in time, prepared them for publication. The journal identifies her as the author. In a more modern setting, the byline might have been: "by Major George Bernard Erath, as told to his daughter Lucy A. Erath."

Source: Lucy A. Erath, "Memoirs of Major George Bernard Erath, II," *The Southwestern Historical Quarterly* 26, no. 4 (April 1923), pp. 263-69.

The announcement of the decision to fight acted like electricity. Being ever ready, our lines were formed at once, but in the low ground out of sight of the Mexicans. Perhaps, a delay of half an hour occurred till the position was perfect as to rank and number. We deployed on the high ground; first in line was the cavalry on the right, the artillery next, the small detachment of regulars next, the first regiment to which I belonged next, and the second regiment commanded by Colonel Sherman on the extreme left.…

…We would have fought the whole world then. We had been marched from the Guadalupe in a round-about, zigzag way through swamps and bogs; we had lived part of the time on half-spoiled beef; we had been delayed in going through the lower country, often standing knee-deep in water waiting on baggage wagons to be drawn out of bogs; we had the experience of having even a woman draw a gun on us — some of us — for confiscating her oxen under orders; and we had been subjected to all the military discipline and practices that were ever enforced on troops of any country, standing guard twenty-four hours out of forty-eight, and not allowed to go to sleep even at the guard fire. General Houston made us a speech at Harrisburg as we started on our march to attack the Mexicans; he promised us that we should have full satisfaction for all we had gone through; and he closed his address by saying let your war cry be "Remember the Alamo!"

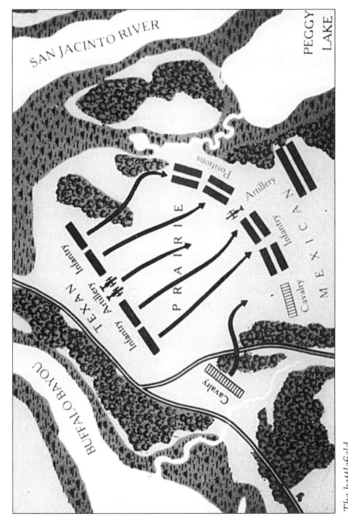

The battlefield

As the Mexicans shot high, nearly all the harm done to us was done during the descent of the hill to the Mexican line. We reserved our fire. It seemed to me that the order to fire was premature, as we were one hundred and fifty yards, I thought, from the Mexicans. While reloading my gun after my first fire I choked the ball. A young man named Ed Blakey was mortally wounded higher up the hill; he ran along by my side until he fell; I picked up his gun and shot bag, and threw mine down. The whole Mexican line was in full flight by the time I got a second shot. Our men advanced rather in disorder, and drove the Mexicans across the boggy slew [swampy area] where many fell.

Their cannon had been taken and passed. Ours had ceased firing because we were too closely mixed with the Mexicans. At a point of timber across the slew, which was by this time bridged with bogged horses on which we crossed, a Mexican officer of high rank, flourishing his sword, made a grand appeal to rally his men, but was shot down, and the men who had turned to face us again resumed their flight only to be overtaken and shot. I do not like to dwell on these scenes. No doubt our men were justifiable, as the Mexican nation deserved punishment for its perfidy, though the soldiers were not responsible for it. About half of them were killed; some drowned in the bay....

Of the main proceedings during the night I know little, being detached from the main body to guard Santa Anna's baggage. I wish to make one further comment on that time, which is, that I believe the Mexican soldiers we encountered that day were much braver than they have ever been credited with being; no one has ever disputed the bravery of their officers....

When Burleson's regiment had slowly assembled,...the right of it was by a pile of baggage closely covering a square of about thirty feet with open spaces inside. It was near the center of what had been the Mexican camp, and about fifty yards away down hill on the bank of the slew was another such square of baggage. The officers had waited till after sundown for men to come in and now Burleson ordered them to take up the march back to camp. I and an elderly man, Simmons, from Bastrop, were at the time standing by this pile of baggage. Burleson came up to me and said, "You two stay right here tonight. Take charge particularly of this pile of baggage, but look after both. You may take anything to eat and allow others to have eatables; but don't let anything valuable be carried off by anybody."...He rode away; we went inside the baggage pile and found it was Santa Anna's, containing camp furniture of silver, nicely arranged, such as a European prince might take with him into the field. And there were besides all kinds of eatables — a considerable part already cooked. Simmons took a kind of mat off a pyramid about six feet high, and called me to look. It was several dozen baskets of champagne; and just beside it was found another such a pyramid. I was not interested in champagne, nor did Simmons make any immoderate use of it; but he gave the bottles liberally to the stragglers returning to camp, saying that it belonged to the eatables which we had permission to give away.

There was a disagreeable scene near; a pile of dead Mexicans, and some wounded ones lay close up against the baggage and among it. Their cries of *A Dios*! and *Agua*! aroused my sympathy and I furnished them with water; but they all died before midnight.

When Captain Roman of Company A of our regiment arrived... he said he had been sent especially to take charge of the military chest the colonel had left in our possession. I told him it was not here but might be in the other pile of baggage which we had not examined; so he marched his company to the other baggage, found the chest, and came back to tell us, when we showed him the champagne. Then he called for his lieutenant, and the matter of champagne got out some way so that we had plenty of company of officers for the rest of the night. I don't think much of the wine was left. I took my carouse [celebratory drink] in eating sugar while others drank. Neither Simmons nor I got a wink of sleep the whole night....

The military chest contained eleven thousand dollars in specie.

Santa Anna's fine saddle, which was in my possession that night, brought eight hundred dollars when sold at auction the next day. All the finery and silver with the military chest brought sixteen hundred dollars. After three thousand was voted to the navy, there was left for every man in the service, whether in the battle or not, eleven dollars apiece. I do not believe the rumors of embezzlement. It is my opinion that everything was handled fairly and squarely....

...In the afternoon I heard a rumor of Santa Anna's capture, and went down to General Houston's camp near the bank of the bayou. Quite in contrast with Santa Anna's extravagant luxuries, Houston lay wounded on a blanket or two, with his head against a tree, and a rope was stretched around him breast high to keep him from being stepped on by passers-by. Santa Anna was already inside the rope, but few were aware that he was there. Lieutenant Bryan and Vice-President Zavalla were interpreting. Almonte, who spoke English well, was also brought....I followed very closely his phrasing in his own language, and thought him a great diplomatist. Among his first propositions was an armistice, and when he understood it was not desired, unless for the purpose of negotiation for our independence, the substance of his reply, as I remember it, was that the fate of war had decided the matter, and he intimated that he would not be averse to granting it. I also remember that he laid stress on the fact that he still had four thousand men under arms on the Brazos, but offered for the sake of compromise to order them to retire....

We were forced to occupy the position nearly a week to dispose of property. As the Mexicans were not buried, the place became disagreeable; we moved three miles higher up. Generals Houston and Santa Anna were taken down to Lynchburg on a steamboat. General Woll [a Mexican officer] came in about the last of April under a flag of truce to attend to the ratification of the terms settled on by the negotiations with Santa Anna.

Perry Alsbury was one of six volunteers from Captain Henry Karnes's cavalry company who joined "Deaf" Smith in the mission to destroy Vince's Bridge. They returned in time for the main battle, which turned out to be very brief, and Alsbury was soon in the chase after Santa Anna. Over two decades later, he wrote the letter from which the following selection has been excerpted.

Source: Alsbury to Weeks, Duncan, and Maveric[k], October 1, 1859, Y. P. Alsbury, "Reminiscences, 1859, 1860," unpublished manuscript, The Center for American History, The University of Texas at Austin. Courtesy of The Center for American History, The University of Texas at Austin.

In a conversation I had the pleasure of holding with you some time since, you expressed an earnest wish to learn from my humble pen all the particular circumstances and incidents that came under my personal observation Relative to the Capture of Genl St. Anna in the Battle Plains of San Jacinto.…

In the first place, I will call your attention to an assersion of opinion I expressed in the naration I addressed to the Hon. Jesse Grimes some two years since Respecting the burning of the Bridge over Vinces Byoue, as an enterprise that led to the capture of St. Anna.

How far I am correct in that opinion, I leave you to judge, from subsequent events, which I will here give you in detail.…

…[T]he wished for order came to make a general Charge, and at the same moment, the Crowd of [Mexican] officers I have spoken off, dashed off of the field, bearing in the direction of the Bridge, the Mexican Cavelry droping in their rear, not stoping even a momant to meet the brunt of our charge, which was by no means marked for its modesty, or Regular order for I do assure you, that in the heat of the charge, in a few minutes, evry officer became a private, and evry private became his own officer, — managing his horse and arms wherever he thought he could do the most execution.…

This is as near as I can tell you the condition of our Cavelry at the time the rout of the Enemy became general; at which time thirteen of us remained together and directed our whole attention to the persuit of their Cavelry, believing as we did, the fact that St. Anna

Charles Shaw, Destroying Vince's Bridge, ca. late 1980s, oil painting

was among them, each one of us eagerly bent forward in his persuit. ...[A]fter reaching a point of elivated ground, about six hundred yds, south of the Battle Ground...he cast a look back over the field, and seeing all was lost, he gave orders to his party, not to push too close on him, and dashed off again, in the direction of the burnt Bridge, — the moment St. Anna ordered a halt, an order I heard and understood, Capt. Carns [Karnes], believing they intended to rally upon us, hatted [halted], and seeing but twelve of us around him he stormed out at the full pich of his voice, to the remainder of his command to come up.

I am certain they did not hear his order, if they did, it was like speaking to so many tempestious billows, each bent upon his own course.

But a moment elapsed, and again we were bending forward, eagerly pressing his rear, as they strung out according to the respective speed of their horses,...from that time, ever an on, until we reached the smoking ruins of Vinces Bridge, we cut them down in detail, reducing their No: to about twenty, a distance of about nine miles, but still, onward he [Santa Anna] rode, with apparent ease, on the swift and splendid black stallion belonging to Mr. Vince little dreaming at the time of the net before him, that had been prepaired to receive him....

Most of their numbers sprang their horses in to the Byoue...[and were] shot by us from the near bank, litterally redening the sluggish stream with human gore.

But one of their number succeeded in getting his horse up the low, boggy bank, and as he mounted the butiful Grey animal, Lieut James Cooke gave him a mortal wound.

he, however rode off at full speed, and reached the Mexican Division that night at Fort Bend, now called Richmond, on the Brazos, — bearing the first news of their dismal defeat....

...St. Anna and three companions were consealed in a small cluster of low bushes within 40 steps of us, and afterwards stated, they heard evry word my brother spoke [calling in Spanish for surrender], they also stated that some altercation took place betwn St. Anna and Genl Cos which was carried on in a whisper.

St. Anna, argued, the only chance left them for life, was to make their way back to our camp, and throw themselves upon the mercy and magnanimity of Genl. Houston a course St. Anna persued, or was persuing, when Mr. Gylfister in company with [Miles] of Capt Fishers Co came across him, next day, April 22nd, and from all I could learn, about two miles from camp, and near the Road leading them to, — my informant also stated, from what he could understand, St. Anna requested to be conducted to Genl Houstons quarters, a request they complied with, little dreaming at the time of the fact, that they were walking with such distinguished company, nor did they know, until the observations of the Prisoners told the secret, as they walked through camp to the Genl Quarters,

Thus, ends the chapter of all the most important facts that I distinctly reccollect as being connected with the capture of the once proud

Dictator of Mexico....

I [do not] wish, to claim, either for myself, or companions, any undue assendency of credit, or honour in the Capture of that distinguished Individual, but rest assured, of one incontrovertable fact, that the distruction of the Bridge over Vinces Byoue, in the first place, pronounced the centence and immediately afterwards, unhorseing him, at the same Bridge, sealed his fate, as a suplicating Prisioner in the hands of my Country....

And strange to tell, a fact that reflects credit upon our Enemies, that during the whole chaise, and struggle of the evening before, I do not reccollect of a single instance of one calling for quarters, they fell, either defending themselves, or trying to escape.

I do not state their number; for the reason I do not reccollet; I believe they were variously estimated from sixty to eighty strong, I am of Deaf Smiths opinion, Texas, at that period had no time to stop to count Enemies; either dead or living.

Colonel Pedro Delgado, one of Santa Anna's aides, barely escaped the Texas cavalry thrust on April 20th. His report is the most evenhanded Mexican account.

Source: Pedro Delgado, "Mexican Account of the Battle of San Jacinto," presented in John J. Linn, *Reminiscences of Fifty Years in Texas* (New York: D. & J. Sadlier & Co, 1883), pp. 225-44.

Paragraph by paragraph, Linn's presentation sets off Delgado's words with quotation marks; this presentation omits them.

On the 14th of April, 1836, his excellency the president [Santa Anna] ordered his staff to prepare to march [from Fort Bend]...leaving his own and the officers' baggage with General Ramirez y Sesma, who was instructed to remain at the crossing of the Brazos....

On the 15th...about noon, we reached a plantation abundantly supplied with corn, meal, sheep, and hogs; it had a good garden and a fine cotton-gin. We halted to refresh men and beasts.

At three o'clock P. M., after having set fire to the dwelling and gin-house, we resumed our march. Here his excellency started ahead with his staff and escort....We travelled at a brisk trot at least ten leagues without halting, until we reached the vicinity of Harrisburg at about eleven o'clock at night. His excellency, with an adjutant and fifteen dragoons, went afoot to that town, distant about one mile, entered it, and succeeded in capturing two Americans, who stated that Zavala and other members of the so-called government of Texas had left the morning before for Galveston....

On the opposite side of the bayou we found two or three houses well supplied with wearing apparel, mainly for women's use, fine furniture, an excellent piano, jars of preserves, chocolate, fruit, etc., all of which was appropriated for the use of his excellency and his attendants. I and others obtained only what they could not use. After the houses had been sacked and burned down a party of Americans fired upon our men from the woods. It is wonderful that some of us...were not killed....

On the 17th, at about three P. M., his excellency, after instructing me to burn the town, started for New Washington with the troops. It was nearly dark when we finished crossing the bayou....

At noon [on the 18th] we reached New Washington, where we found flour, soap, tobacco, and other articles, which were issued to the men. His excellency instructed me to mount one of his horses, and with a small party of dragoons to gather beeves for the use of the troops. In a short time I drove in over one hundred head of cattle, so abundant are they in that country....

On the 20th...we had burnt a fine warehouse on the wharf and all the houses in the town when Captain Barragan rushed in at full speed, reporting that Houston was close on our rear, and that his troops had captured some of our stragglers....

It was two o'clock P. M. when we descried Houston's pickets at the edge of a large wood in which he concealed his main force. Our skirmishers commenced firing, when they were answered by the enemy, who fell back into the wood. His excellency reached the ground with the main body, with the intention, as I understood, of attacking at once; but they kept hidden, which kept him from ascertaining their position.

He therefore changed his dispositions and ordered the company of Toluca to deploy as skirmishers in the direction of the woods....

...Then his excellency went to look for a camping-ground, and established his whole force along the shore of San Jacinto Bay....

At length, at five o'clock P. M., my duty was performed, and as I entered the camp with the last load I was closely followed by the enemy's cavalry. His excellency, noticing it, instructed me to order Captain Aguirre, who commanded our cavalry, to face the enemy without gaining ground. This movement checked the enemy for a few moments; but soon after they dashed upon our dragoons and were close enough to engage them with the sword, without, however, any material result.

Then his excellency, deploying several companies as skirmishers, forced the enemy back to his camp, on which he retired sluggishly and in disorder. This engagement took place after sundown. At daybreak on the 21st his excellency ordered a breastwork to be erected for the cannon. It was constructed with pack-saddles, sacks of hard-bread, baggage, etc. A trifling barricade of branches ran along its front and right....

We had the enemy on our right in a wood at long musket-range. Our front, although level, was exposed to the fire of the enemy, who could keep it up with impunity from his sheltered position. Retreat was easy for him on his rear and right, while our own troops had no space for manoeuvring. We had in our rear a small grove, reaching to the bay shore, which extended on our right as far as New Washington. What ground had we to retreat upon in case of a reverse? From sad experience I answer, none!

A few hours before the engagment I submitted to General Castrillon a few remarks on the subject, suggested by my limited knowledge; but he answered: *'What can I do, my friend? I know it well, but I cannot help it. You know that nothing avails here against the caprice, arbitrary will, and ignorance of that man!'*

This was said in an impassioned voice and in close proximity to his excellency's tent.

At 9 o'clock A.M. General Cos came in with a reinforcement of about five hundred men. His arrival was greeted by the roll of drums and with joyful shouts. As it was represented to his excellency that these men had not slept the night before, he instructed them to stack their arms, to remove their accoutrements, and to go to sleep quietly in the adjoining grove.

No important incident took place until half-past four P.M. At this fatal moment, the bugler on the right signaled the enemy's advance upon that wing. His excellency and staff were asleep. The greater number of the men were also sleeping. Of the rest, some were eating, others were scattered in the woods in search of boughs to prepare shelter. Our line was composed of musket-stacks. Our cavalry were riding bareback to and from water. I stepped upon some ammunition-boxes the better to observe the movements of the enemy. I saw that their formation was a mere line in one rank, and very extended. In their centre was the Texas flag. On both wings they had two light cannons, well manned. Their cavalry was opposite our front, overlapping our left. In this disposition, yelling furiously, with a brisk fire of grape, muskets, and rifles, they advanced resolutely upon our camp. There the utmost confusion prevailed. General Castrillon shouted on one side; on another Colonel Almonte was giving orders; some cried out to commence firing, others to lie down to avoid the grape shot. Among the latter was his excellency.

Then already I saw our men flying in small groups, terrified, and sheltering themselves behind large trees. I endeavored to force some of them to fight, but all efforts were in vain; the evil was beyond remedy. They were a bewildered, panic-stricken herd.

The enemy kept up a brisk cross-fire of grape on the woods. Presently we heard in close proximity the unpleasant noise of their clamors.

Meeting no resistance, they dashed lightning-like upon our deserted camp.

Then I saw his excellency running about in the utmost excitement, wringing his hands and unable to give an order. General Castrillon was stretched upon the ground, wounded in the leg. Colonel Trevino was killed, and Colonel Marcial Aguirre was severely wounded. I saw also the enemy reaching the ordnance train and killing a corporal and two gunners who had been detailed to repair cartridges which had been damaged on the previous evening. Everything was lost. I went, leading my horse — which I could not mount, as the firing had rendered him restless and fractious — to join our men, still hoping that we might be able to defend ourselves or to retire under shelter of the night. This, however, could not be done. It is a known fact that Mexican soldiers, once demoralized, cannot be controlled unless they are thoroughly inured to war. On the left, and about a musket-shot distant from our camp, was a small grove on the bay shore. Our disbanded herd rushed for it to obtain shelter from the horrid slaughter carried on all over the prairie by the bloodthirsty usurpers. Unfortunately we met in our way an obstacle hard to overcome. It was a bayou, not very wide, but rather deep. The men, on reaching it, would hopelessly crowd together, and were shot down by the enemy, who was close enough to not miss his aim. It was there that the greatest carnage took place.

Upon reaching that spot I saw Colonel Almonte swimming across

41

the bayou with his left hand, and holding up his right, which grasped his sword. I stated before that I was leading my horse, but, at this critical situation I vaulted upon him, and with two leaps he landed me on the opposite side of the bayou. To my sorrow I had to leave the noble animal mired in that place, and to part with him probably for ever.

As I dismounted, I sank into the mire waist deep, and I had the greatest trouble to get out of it by catching hold of the grass. Both my shoes remained in the bayou. I made an effort to recover them, but I came to the conclusion that did I tarry there a rifle shot would make an outlet for my soul, as had happened to many a poor fellow around me. Thus I made for the grove barefooted.

There I met a number of other officers, with whom I wandered at random, buried in gloomy thoughts upon our tragic disaster.

We still entertained a hope of rallying some of the men, but it was impossible.

The enemy's cavalry surrounded the grove, while his infantry penetrated it, pursuing us with fierce and bloodthirsty feelings....

Thence they marched us to their camp. I was barefooted; the prairie had recently been burned, and the stubble, hardened by the fire, penetrated like needles the soles of my feet, so that I could scarcely walk. This did not prevent them from striking me with the butt end of their guns because I did not walk as fast as they wished. These savages struck with their bayonets our wounded soldiers lying on the way; others following them consummated the sacrifice by a musket or a pistol shot....

After keeping us sitting there [in camp] about an hour and a half they marched us into the woods, where we saw an immense fire....

I and several of my companions were silly enough to believe that we were about to be burnt alive in retaliation for those who had been burnt in the Alamo....However, we felt considerably relieved when they placed us around the fire to warm ourselves and to dry our wet clothes. We were surrounded by twenty-five or thirty sentinels. You should have seen those men, or rather phantoms, converted into moving armories. Some wore two, three, and even four brace of pistols, a cloth bag of very respectable size filled with bullets, a powder-horn, a sabre or a bowie-knife, besides a rifle, a musket, or carbine. Every one of them had in his hand a burning candle....Was this display of light intended to prevent us from attempting to escape? The fools! Where could we go in that vast country, unknown to us, intersected by large rivers and forests, where wild beasts and hunger, and where they themselves, would destroy us?...

At two o'clock P. M. [on the 22d] his excellency the General-in-Chief, Don Antonio Lopez de Santa Anna, arrived, under the charge of a mounted soldier. He wore linen trousers, a blue cotton jacket, a cap, and red worsted slippers. His leader did not know him, but, noticing a movement of curiosity amongst us as he approached, he became satisfied that he was conducting no common officer, and reported at once with him to General Houston. The latter sent two of his adjutants to inquire of us whether Santa Anna had lost any teeth. Some answered that they did not know, but others, with more candor, or perhaps less discretion, said: 'Yes, gentlemen; and you can further say to your general that the person just brought before him is President Santa Anna himself.' The news spread over the whole camp, and the inquisitive fellows who surrounded us ran to strike up an acquaintance with his excellency. Some of them proposed to fire salutes and to make other demonstrations to celebrate the capture of so lofty a personage; but Houston courteously forbade it. From this time we were left alone, his excellency having become the centre of attraction.

On the 23d seventy or eighty loads of ordnance-stores had been brought in and deposited, together with piles of loaded muskets and cartridge-boxes, in close proximity to our camp. We had noticed repeatedly that some of the Americans went about that combustible matter, and even handled it, with their pipes in their mouths. In one of these instances of carelessness some grains of powder scattered on the ground were ignited. The fire reached the cartridge-boxes and their contents, and soon extended to the pans of the muskets, which exploded like an infernal machine. The prairie, too, was set on fire, and the covers of the ordnance-boxes were already burning. Those nearest to the scene of danger took to flight. We and our sentinels followed....Then the guard and some of the officers, in view of the increasing danger, chose not to remain hindmost, and kept pace with us, expecting at every moment the fatal explosion. We had run a considerable distance when we turned and looked back, and discovered that the fire had been extinguished. We could not help applauding the resolution and bold determination with which some of these extraordinary men had rushed into the flames and smothered them with their feet and blankets and some water from the bay. We had a narrow escape. I thought at one time that the conquerors of San Jacinto would all be blown up into eternity; not, however, without some regret on my part to have to go the way they went, owing to their stupid carelessness....

[On the 24th] a steamboat arrived, having on board the Texan president, Vice-President Zavala, and other members of the administration....

On the 26th our property was sold at auction. It was hard to see them breaking our trunks open and every one of them loaded with our shirts, trousers, coats, etc., while we remained with what we had on our bodies. I saw my boots going, while my blistered feet were wrapped in pieces of rawhide....

On the 27th and following days no incident took place worth being noticed. I will only say, to the lasting shame of our conquerors, that they kept us starving, sleeping in the mud, and exposed to frequent and heavy showers. Still more intolerable was the stench rising from the corpses on the field of San Jacinto, which they had not the generosity to burn or bury after the time-honored custom, regardless of their own comfort and health and those of the surrounding settlements. On the 3d of May, at four o'clock P.M., we were sent to another camp, distant a little over one league....On the 7th, at five o'clock P.M., they marched us on board the steamboat *Yellowstone*, where we found General Santa Anna, the president, Señor Zavala, and other dignitaries of their so-called government.

Shortly afterwards General Houston was carried on board on his cot, on his way to New Orleans to obtain medical attendance for a wound received in the leg at the battle of San Jacinto....

Report of the Victorious General

Sam Houston, as commanding officer, wrote an official report while waiting to leave the San Jacinto battlefield to obtain treatment for his severely wounded ankle.

Source: Sam Houston, "Official Report of the Battle of San Jacinto," in *The Writings of Sam Houston, 1813-1863*, vol 1, edited by Amelia W. Williams and Eugene C. Barker (Austin: The University of Texas Press, 1938), pp. 416-20.

Headquarters of the Army, San Jacinto, April 25, 1836.

To David G. Burnet, President of the Republic of Texas:

Sir: I regret extremely that my situation, since the battle of the 21st, has been such as to prevent my rendering you my official report of the same previous to this time.

I have the honor to inform you that, on the evening of the 18th inst., after a forced march of fifty-five miles, which was effected in two days and half, the army arrived opposite Harrisburg. That evening a courier of the enemy was taken, from whom I learned that General Santa Anna, with one division of his choice troops, had marched in the direction of Lynch's ferry, on the San Jacinto — burning Harrisburg as he passed down.

The army was ordered to be in readiness to march early on the next morning. The main body effected a crossing over Buffalo bayou, below Harrisburg, on the morning of the 19th, having left the baggage, the sick, and a sufficient camp-guard in the rear. We continued the march through the night, making but one halt in the prairie for a short time, and without refreshments. At daylight we resumed the line of march, and in a short distance our scouts encountered those of the enemy, and we received information that General Santa Anna was at New Washington, and would that day take up the line of

Stephen Seymour Thomas, The Equestrian, *1892, oil painting depicting Sam Houston*

march for Anahuac, crossing at Lynch's ferry. The Texan army halted within half a mile of the ferry, in some timber and were engaged in slaughtering beeves, when the army of Santa Anna was discovered to be approaching in battle array, having been encamped at Clopper's point, eight miles below. Disposition was immediately made of our forces, and preparation for his reception. He took a position with his infantry, and artillery in the centre, occupying an island of timber, his cavalry covering the left flank. The artillery, consisting of one double-fortified medium brass twelve-pounder, then opened on our encampment. The infantry, in column, advanced with the design of charging our lines, but were repulsed by a discharge of grape and canister from our artillery, consisting of two six-pounders. The enemy had occupied a piece of timber within rifle-shot of the left wing of our army, from which an occasional interchange of small-arms took place between the troops, until the enemy withdrew to a position on the bank of the San Jacinto, about three quarters of a mile from our encampment, and commenced fortification.

A short time before sunset, our mounted men, about eighty-five in number, under the special command of Colonel Sherman, marched out for the purpose of reconnoitring the enemy. While advancing they received a volley from the left of the enemy's infantry, and after a sharp re-encounter with their cavalry, in which ours acted extremely well and performed some feats of daring chivalry, they retired in good order, having had two men severely wounded, and several horses killed. In the meantime, the infantry under the command of Lieutenant-Colonel Millard, and Colonel Burleson's regiment, with the artillery, had marched out for the purpose of covering the retreat of the cavalry, if necessary. All then fell back in good order to our encampment about sunset, and remained without ostensible action until the 21st, at half-past three o'clock, taking the first refreshment which they had enjoyed for two days. The enemy in the meantime extended the right flank of their infantry, so as to occupy the extreme point of a skirt of timber on the bank of the San Jacinto, and secured their left by a fortification about five feet high, constructed of packs and baggage, leaving an opening in the centre of the breastwork, in which their artillery was placed, their cavalry upon their left wing.

About nine o'clock on the morning of the 21st, the enemy were reinforced by five hundred choice troops, under the command of General Cos, increasing their effective force to upward of fifteen hundred men, while our aggregate force for the field numbered seven hundred and eighty-three. At half-past three o'clock in the evening, I ordered the officers of the Texan army to parade their respective commands, having in the meantime ordered the bridge on the only road communicating with the Bra[z]os, distance eight miles from our encampment, to be destroyed — thus cutting off all possibility of escape. Our troops paraded with alacrity and spirit, and were anxious for the contest. Their conscious disparity in numbers seemed only to increase their enthusiasm and confidence, and heightened their anxiety for the contest. Our situation afforded me an opportunity of making the arrangements preparatory to the attack without exposing our designs to the enemy. The *first* regiment, commanded by Colonel Burleson, was assigned to the centre. The *second* regiment, under the command of Colonel Sherman, formed the left wing of the army. The artillery, under the special command of Colonel George W. Hockley, inspector-general, was placed on the right of the first regiment; and four companies of infantry, under the command of Lieutenant-Colonel Henry Millard, sustained the artillery upon the right. Our cavalry, sixty-one in number, commanded by Colonel Mirabeau B. Lamar (whose gallant and daring conduct on the previous day had attracted the admiration of his comrades, and called him to that station), placed on our extreme right, completed our line. Our cavalry was first despatched to the front of the enemy's left, for the purpose of attracting their notice, while an extensive island of timber afforded us an opportunity of concentrating our forces and deploying from that point, agreeably to the previous design of the troops. Every evolution was performed with alacrity, the whole advancing rapidly in line, through an open prairie, without any protection whatever for our men. The artillery advanced and took station within two hundred yards of the enemy's breastwork, and commenced an effective fire with grape and canister.

Colonel Sherman, with his regiment, having commenced the action upon our left wing, the whole line, at the centre and on the right, advancing in double quick time, raised the war cry, "*Remember the Alamo!*" received the enemy's fire, and advanced within point-blank shot, before a piece was discharged from our lines. Our line advanced without a halt, until they were in possession of the woodland and the enemy's breastwork — the right wing of Burleson's and the left of Millard's taking possession of the breastwork; our artillery having gallantly charged up within seventy yards of the enemy's cannon, when it was taken by our troops.

The conflict lasted about eighteen minutes from the time of close action until we were in possession of the enemy's encampment, taking one piece of cannon (loaded), four stand of colors, all their camp equipage, stores, and baggage. Our cavalry had charged and routed that of the enemy upon the right, and given pursuit to the fugitives, which did not cease until they arrived at the bridge which I have mentioned before — Captain Karnes, always among the foremost in danger, commanding the pursuers. The conflict in the breastwork lasted but a few moments; many of the troops encountered hand to hand, and, not having the advantage of bayonets on our side, our riflemen used their pieces as war-clubs, breaking many of them off at the breech. The rout commenced at half-past four, and the pursuit by the main army continued until twilight. A guard was then left in charge of the enemy's encampment, and our army returned with their killed and wounded. In the battle, our loss was two killed and twenty-three wounded, six of them mortally. The enemy's loss was six hundred and thirty killed, among whom was one general officer, four colonels, two lieutenant-colonels, five captains, twelve lieutenants; wounded, two hundred and eight, of which were five colonels, three lieutenant-colonels, two second-lieutenant colonels, seven captains, one cadet; prisoners seven hundred and thirty — President-General Santa Anna, General Cos, four colonels, aides to General Santa Anna, and the colonel of the Guerrero battalion, are included in the number. General Santa Anna was not taken until the 22nd, and General Cos yesterday, very few having escaped. About six hundred muskets, three hundred sabres, and two hundred pistols, have been collected since the action. Several hundred mules and horses were taken, and nearly twelve thousand dollars in specie.

For several days previous to the action, our troops were engaged in forced marches, exposed to excessive rains, and the additional inconvenience of extremely bad roads, badly supplied with rations and clothing; yet, amid every difficulty, they bore up with cheerfulness and fortitude, and performed their marches with spirit and alacrity — there was no murmuring.

Previous to and during the action, my staff evinced every disposition to be useful, and were actively engaged in their duties. In the conflict I am assured that they demeaned themselves in such a manner as proved them worthy members of the Army of San Jacinto. Colonel T. J. Rusk, secretary of war, was on the field. For weeks his services had been highly beneficial to the army. In the battle, he was on the left wing, where Colonel Sherman's command first encountered and drove in the enemy: he bore himself gallantly, and continued his efforts and activity, remaining with the pursuers until resistance ceased.

I have the honor of transmitting herewith a list of all the officers and men who were engaged in the action, which I respectfully request may be published, as an act of justice to the individuals. For the commanding general to attempt discrimination as to the conduct of those who commanded in the action, or those who were commanded, would be impossible. Our success in the action is conclusive proof of their daring intrepidity and courage; every officer and man proved himself worthy of the cause in which he battled, while the triumph received a lustre from the humanity which characterized their conduct after victory, and richly entitles them to the admiration and gratitude of their general. Nor should we withhold the tribute of our grateful thanks from that Being who rules the destinies of nations, and has, in the time of greatest need, enabled us to arrest a powerful invader while devastating our country.

Sam Houston, *Commander-in-Chief.*

Retreat of the Mexican Army

After his capture at San Jacinto, Santa Anna dispatched orders to his second in command, General Vicente Filisola, to retreat with all troops. Filisola followed the orders and received substantial criticism in Mexico for doing so, his critics contending that Santa Anna had hardly been in a position to issue those orders freely.

Source: H[enderson K.] Yoakum, *History of Texas from Its First Settlement in 1685 to Its Annexation to the United States in 1846*, vol. 2 (New York: Redfield, 1856), pp. 149-50.

"ARMY OF OPERATIONS.

"EXCELLENT SIR: Having yesterday evening, with the small division under my immediate command, had an encounter with the enemy, which, notwithstanding I had previously taken all possible precautions, proved unfortunate, I am, in consequence, a prisoner in the hands of the enemy. Under these circumstances, your excellency will order General Gaona with his division to countermarch to Bexar, and wait for orders. Your excellency will also, with the division under your immediate command, march to the same place. The division under command of General Urrea will retire to Guadalupe Victoria. I have agreed with General Houston for an armistice, until matters can be so regulated that the war shall cease for ever.

"Your excellency will take the proper steps for the support of the army, which from this time remains under your command, using the moneys lately arrived from Matamoras, the provisions on hand there, as well as those at Victoria, and also the twenty thousand dollars withdrawn from Bexar, and are now in that treasury.

"I hope your excellency will, without failure, comply with these dispositions — advising me, by return of the courier, that you have already commenced their execution. God and liberty !

"Camp at San Jacinto, April 22, 1836.

"ANT°. LOPEZ DE SANTA ANNA.

"To his Excellency Don VICENTE FILISOLA, *General of Division.*"

De la Peña, a junior Mexican officer, participated in the battle at the Alamo but missed San Jacinto because orders had kept him some distance up the Brazos River, in the vicinity of Old Fort (Thompson's) and Fort Bend. Never happy with the leadership in the campaign, he was in disbelief at his army's retreat.

Source: José Enrique de la Peña, *With Santa Anna in Texas: A Personal Narrative of the Revolution,* translated and edited by Carmen Perry with an introduction by Llerena Friend (College Station: Texas A&M University Press, 1975), pp. 116-33. Reprinted by permission of Texas A&M University Press.

Old Fort, April 22nd....

General Gaona...arrived yesterday with his brigade at this general headquarters, and he has been reinforced with the rest of the Guadalajara Battalion....Today his brigade began to cross to the other side in order to continue his march toward Nacogdoches, and when I emerged from the woods between two and three in the afternoon, I came close to the river crossing and found that the part of the brigade that had already crossed was crossing back again. Everyone was asking the cause of this countermovement, and no one could give a reason, but at five in the afternoon rumors are circulating that the commander in chief was defeated yesterday....[I]f the rumor is confirmed, the only surprise to me would be that it had not happened before, given the disorder with which the commander in chief has led us, with his errors and aberrations....Up to now the enemy has not known how to conduct the war, and this has saved us....

Sunday the 24th of April. This is an unknown plain where we arrived between two and three o'clock in the morning....Don Miguel Aguirre, who commanded the general in chief's guard and who returned on the 22nd, is, among others, one of those who affirmed the total destruction of the forces under his own immediate and personal command, together with those which General Cos commanded. According to what this officer says, it is known that the action during which this catastrophe occurred took place on the 21st at four o'clock in the afternoon on the near bank of the San Jacinto, and that there perished in it, by surprise (a surprise at four o'clock in the afternoon!), the Guerrero Battalion…the Aldama…the Matamoros…and the Toluca: almost all in the formation…which had suffered considerable casualties in the Alamo assault.…[B]ut nothing is definitely known because none of those actively engaged in the affray has arrived except Aguirre, who is wounded, and a few soldiers and domestics.

The night of the 22nd the Sapper Battalion received orders to approach the banks of the river, and we commanders and officers were under the impression that we were going on the offensive to hold the crossing while the rest of the army went over it, a natural assumption; but we occupied the whole bank, not without some surprise and indignation at the recrossing of the loads of ammunition and supplies that had already crossed to the other side during the march under General Gaona.…

Thoughts and sensations of this day. This countermarch is really cruel and harsh to me, for, in my opinion, after effecting a reunion with General Urrea, we should have marched to vindicate the honor of our arms, to avenge our companions, and to save those who might still be alive, but unfortunately only some of the commanders and the majority of the subalterns share this view, for the generals have not even wanted to wait for the stragglers who might rejoin us, when General Santa Anna might perhaps be one of them.…

The 25th.…[T]here arrived…Luis Espinosa, fifer of the Guerrero Battalion, a young man twelve years old and extraordinarily alert, who has given me a detailed narrative of the happenings at San Jacinto and who confirms, as the others have, that the defeat was by surprise and that the greater part of our forces perished.…Espinosa believes that General Santa Anna and his general staff, who had been able to save themselves as far as Buffalo Bayou, have perished.…At every moment I become more convinced that we should have died and died honorably before abandoning the camp to the enemy, burdened with ignominy....

We should note above all that the enemy, disconcerted by the successive victories of our army, terrified by the fall of the Alamo, by Fannin's defeat and the accelerated movements of General Urrea, was seeking safety in retreat, and a well-ordered march would have been the only thing necessary to end the campaign without having to fire another single shot. Were I the most devoted admirer of General Santa Anna, I would not dare to excuse him of the great error committed in venturing to cross to the other side of the Brazos with only 700 men when he could have had General Ramírez y Sesma's full division made up of over 1,400 men, for by delaying the march ten days he could have had with him over 2,000. But the assurances given him by some of the prisoners that the families fleeing from us

Antonio López de Santa Anna, oil painting, artist and date unknown

carried with them valuable assets, and the avarice that has characterized all his actions; the desire to make the campaign as horrible as possible and to end it quickly, so that he could return to the interior to receive homage and to consolidate his power, perhaps for life, according to the news that had leaked out and which I have referred to previously; all these things drove him to act precipitately. This is the more believable as one sees that his advance was by a route where no enemy was to be found, leaving him to the left, although the ostensible object for which he abandoned the general headquarters at Thompson's on the 14th of April was to seize the men who made up the so-called government of Texas, who at that moment were at the town of Harrisburg. It is not credible that this could have been the sole object of his march, because apprehending a handful of men who had no force on hand to defend them would have been an easy task for a cavalry patrol to carry out, since they have fast mobility and would not attract attention, circumstances which would not be as favorable were a division to execute it, no matter how mobile. It would have been more worthy for our commander in chief to advance to meet the enemy than to apprehend those judged to be the leaders of the revolution, something the most insignificant army member could have done....

...General Santa Anna had under his command forces superior in both number and discipline; he had excellent officers, and though there were some recruits in his ranks, these were the lesser number. ...Houston, on the contrary, had forces inferior in number which, though composed of men of courage, were not subject to the discipline that makes the soldier; they did not follow any specific tactics nor had they mastered the fundamentals of war. It can be said of them that they were all recruits, courageous men, who tried only to save or to sell their lives dearly, for which reason the defeat at San Jacinto appears the more humiliating, for in defeat disgrace is quite possible, just as one can be vanquished without necessarily losing honor; but on the 21st of April everything was lost, men, arms, and reputation.

Explanations in Mexico

Santa Anna returned home and defended his actions in a publication in which he blames others for the loss of Texas.

Source: Antonio L[ó]pez de Santa-Anna, *Manifesto which General Antonio Lopez de Santa-Anna Addresses to His Fellow-Citizens Relative to His Operations during the Texas Campaign and His Capture 10 of May 1837*, presented in *The Mexican Side of the Texas Revolution [1836]*, translated with notes by Carlos E. Castañeda (Dallas: P. L. Turner Company, 1928; reprint, New York: Arno Press, 1976), pp. 5-38.

NEVER has the ambitious thought of obtaining universal approval for my actions entered my mind; nor have I been so pusillanimous that the fear of the disapproval of a few, or even of many, could have prevented me from acting in a certain way when convinced, even though erroneously, of the propriety of my action. In the palace of Mexico as in this humble hut, in the midst of the applause of a free people the same as amidst the insolent hisses of the Texans who loudly called for my death, I have realized that my conduct would always be criticized, for who has not at least one enemy if fate has raised him above his fellow-citizens and placed him in the public eye? I was not surprised, therefore, to see the triumphs of Béxar and the Alamo tainted by the tireless and venomous tooth of that envy which I have always despised, nor the defeat of San Jacinto horribly portrayed by the unfaithful and disloyal brush of an unjust animosity; much less was I surprised that by these means a great part of a nation, zealous as it should be of its honor and anxious that the cost of sustaining it should be reduced to a minimum, should have been made to doubt the propriety of my war measures if not to condemn them outright....

...I had sworn that my sword should always be the first to strike the blow upon the daring necks of her [Mexico's] enemies, and the news that came from Texas regarding the plight of General Don Martín Cós, besieged in Béxar by the Texans, late in 1835, made me realize that they were the most formidable enemies that threatened our country at that time....

...The great problem I had to solve was to reconquer Texas....[I]t was of the utmost importance to prevent the enemy from strengthening its position or receiving the reenforcements that the papers from the North asserted were very numerous....Had we been favored by victory...this policy would have shown a surprised world our occupation, in sixty days, of a territory more than four hundred leagues in extent and defended by the enemy....

[T]he enemy fortified itself in the Alamo....Before undertaking the assault...I offered life to the defendants who would surrender their arms and retire under oath not to take them up again against Mexico....[T]heir decision irrevocably sealed their fate....

...The Alamo was taken...costing us seventy dead and about three hundred wounded....Let us weep at the tomb of the brave Mexicans who died at the Alamo defending the honor and the rights of their country....

The enemy...fled before our forces....

...Few of the colonists, properly speaking, have taken up arms in the struggle. The soldiers of Travis at the Alamo, those of Fannin at Perdido, the riflemen of Dr. Grant, and Houston himself and his troops at San Jacinto, with but few exceptions, were publicly known to have come from New Orleans and other points of the neighboring republic exclusively for the purpose of aiding the Texas rebellion without ever having been members of any of the colonization grants....

At San Felipe de Austin we found only the ashes of what had been a town....The enemy, with the help of a steamboat, had taken refuge at Groce's crossing....I looked for another crossing and succeeded in taking Thompson's [near Fort Bend],...where I ordered the army to reunite....The president, the cabinet members of the so-called government of Texas, and the chief leaders of the revolution were gathered there [in Harrisburg] where a single blow would have been mortal to their cause....

I, therefore, decided to reach Harrisburg by forced marches without waiting for the rest of the army, for I really did not need it to attack a point entirely devoid of troops....In spite of all my diligence, the fear that our blow upon Harrisburg might be frustrated was realized. The town was abandoned....Some printers there were able to tell us only that they had fled towards Galveston....It was of the utmost importance to force a fight and the only way possible was to cut off their retreat....

The printers already mentioned assured me that Houston's force did not exceed 800 men....[I]t was confirmed by...Colonel Almonte from New Washington....That officer succeeded in capturing a large train of supplies from the enemy....His force being so small, I believed it expedient to march to his aid and to insure the safety of the supplies he had captured that were so important for us....I arrived then, at New Washington the 18th of April, having sent, under the command of Captain Marcos Barragán, an advance guard to Lynchburg to observe the movements of the enemy, who...would have to pass in sight of that point, where it was my intention to attack it....I marched upon Lynchburg on the 20th. I had already asked my second in command, His Excellency, General D. Vicente Filisola, to send me five hundred *picked* men with General Martín Cós. I stressed the word *picked* purposely, in order to avoid his sending me the recruits that I well knew made up the greater part of our army. While on the road, Captain Barragán came to inform me that the enemy was approaching Lynchburg....I had the satisfaction of...confirming the information I had of its strength, and of observing that it had taken a disadvantageous position in the low lands of the angle formed by the junction of Buffalo Bayou and the San Jacinto just before they enter Galveston Bay....[I]t never crossed my mind that a moment of rest, now indispensable, should have been so disastrous, particularly after I had issued orders for strict vigilance to insure our safety. It was, however, overconfidence that lulled the zeal of those in whom I trusted. My sleep was interrupted by the noise of arms, and upon awakening I saw with astonishment that the enemy had completely surprised our camp. In vain I tried to repair the evil....I exhausted all my efforts trying to turn the tide....[I]t was too late....

...I made my way through the enemy with the greatest difficulty as far as the head of Buffalo Bayou, beyond which, my retreat would be safe, but pursued constantly, it was impossible for me to reach this last anchor of salvation. A mere accident permitted me, on the following day, to change my wet clothing in an abandoned house where I found some others cast off. To that same good luck I owe my not having attracted the attention of those who pursued us, who a few hours later overtook me and believing that I was an officer of the Mexicans army made me appear before the Chief of the Texans, Sam Houston, on the very battlefield of our engagement....

The first duty during my imprisonment was to demand the treatment and considerations due a prisoner of war....[T]heir effrontery went as far as to demand the practical surrender of the entire army under my command. The idea was as preposterous as it was highly offensive to our national honor, and my indignation must have been shown so clearly in my face that Houston himself blushed and changed the nature of the proposal, contenting himself with the retirement of the army....

...[T]he retreat of General Filisola could have had no other origin than a concept on this point diametrically opposed to mine. Thus in his reply to my communication of the 22nd he said that he was acting only out of consideration for the safety of my person....

Two days would have been sufficient for the forces gathered at Thompson's alone to have given a blow to the enemy that would have repaired easily the misfortune of the 21st....I flatter myself...that if I had been able to reach Thompson's as I wanted, victory would have returned to our troops within three days....

I foresaw, therefore, the confusion of the moment among the troops of our army and I took advantage of the opportunity afforded by Houston's proposal, succeeding...in giving the said army the time necessary for its reorganization as the result of an armistice that I concluded but which our troops used only to retreat unmolested....

In all justice it must be confessed, however, that the Texan general, Sam Houston, is educated and is actuated by humanitarian sentiments. I am indebted to him for a treatment as decorous as the circumstances permitted while he was in Texas, and for my liberty after he returned from New Orleans where he went to have a wound that he received at San Jacinto treated....

Caro, Santa Anna's secretary, did not escape the general finger-pointing by the defeated general and responded point by point in a book published in 1837. Caro made generous use of notes, especially for responding to various of Santa Anna's assertions. The narrative assembled here comes partially from Caro's text and partially from his notes. Passages taken from the notes are presented in smaller type.

Source: Ramón Martínez Caro, *A True Account of the First Texas Campaign and the Events Subsequent to the Battle of San Jacinto* (Mexico: Imprenta de Santiago Perez, 1837), presented in *The Mexican Side of the Texas Revolution [1836],* translated with notes by Carlos E. Castañeda (Dallas: P. L. Turner Company, 1928; reprint, New York: Arno Press, 1976), pp. 93-125.

The evident artfulness of the communications addressed to the supreme government by His Excellency, Antonio López de Santa Anna,...is in keeping with his well-known character of duplicity. It confirms the opinion in which he is generally held as a result of the many deceits he has practiced upon the nation....

[Santa Anna claimed fatigue as his excuse for being asleep when the battle of San Jacinto erupted. Ed.]

...If a general-in-chief, who has been confronted by the enemy for only twenty-four hours, an enemy who on the day before makes a false attack to feel our strength, is forced to lie down and rest from the hardships of one night's vigil, what can be expected from the unfortunate soldiers, really fatigued by the many hardships of the campaign? Can they be blamed if they too, were sleeping at the time of the attack?...

The horrible memory of that moment makes the pen drop from my hand for a few minutes. Imagine our being surprised at four in the afternoon, in the middle of an open plain, with nothing to obstruct the view of the enemy from our front! They succeeded in advancing to within 200 yards from our trenches without being discovered, and from there they spread death and terror among our ranks. This is unpardonable. Our country, our honor, humanity, the shades of the bleeding victims sacrificed by that criminal negligence call for vengeance. The shadows of those who fell, so cowardly murdered, at Refugio, Goliad, and the Alamo had called for vengeance for some time....

Their war cry was "Remember the Alamo."...

[Santa Anna claimed that a servant of his aide-de-camp gave him a horse and urged him to save himself. Ed.]

God forbid that His Excellency should have made his way through the enemy. I was a short distance away — not exactly among the enemy — when I saw him coming already in flight and I followed him immediately. Thank God we were not among the last who fled, for of those very few survived to tell the tale. We continued at full speed until we reached the bridge on the Brazos, eight miles away, but only to find it burned. We retraced our steps a short distance and entered a small thicket, where he dismounted and left me. I followed a path with Lieut. Col. José Maria Castillo Iberri, Capt. Marcos Barragán, and some others whose names I do not recall. They all succeeded in crossing a creek, but I was prevented from following them by the approach of the enemy who was already entering the woods. I turned back and hid among some thick brush. There I remained all night in constant danger of death, for to make things worse it was a full moon night. After daybreak, totally exhausted, I gave myself up to two of the enemy who were passing nearby....

They took me to Houston, whom I found suffering from a wound in his foot....

Houston addressed several questions to me to ascertain the whereabouts of His Excellency, to all of which I truthfully replied that I did not know where he was....

Shortly after the arrival of His Excellency in camp, Mr. Thomas J. Rusk, who was acting as secretary of war for the Texans, came looking for me....I was informed that accompanied by one of Houston's aides I should go back to the battlefield to search for and bring back the portable *escritoire* [writing-desk] and other belongings of the private secretarial staff of His Excellency.

We left for the purpose, taking with us one of our soldiers to bring back whatever we found. To me alone was reserved the sharp pain of beholding our battlefield after the action. The first thing that met my eye...was the sight of General Castrillón where he fell, already stripped of his clothes. A short distance from him and in the same condition I saw the bodies of...other officers...and about fifty soldiers. These were all the dead at this place which had been our battle line. We made our way to the woods, about one hundred paces away, and upon our arrival there, the soldier we had brought had already found His Excellency's *escritoire*....

...As we started back, I told him that I did not believe the number of the dead was as large as it was claimed, for both on our battle line and in our immediate vicinity the dead did not exceed one hundred. Wishing to satisfy my doubts, he led me to the entrance of the road taken by our troops in their flight, and there I saw, both to the right and to the left, as far as the eye could see, a double file of corpses, all men from our force. Moved by this sad spectacle...I still had the more bitter sorrow of being conducted a short distance to the left, where there was a small creek, at the edge of the woods, where the bodies were so thickly piled upon each other that they formed a bridge across it....I turned my face in horror; and...he repeated, "Let us go." "Yes," I replied, "take me away from this place." We made our way back to where the soldier was with the *escritoire*, and he told me that he had seen both His Excellency's and my own bed a short distance away. I asked for permission to take them back to camp, and this being granted...we returned to Houston's presence.

Thanks to this lucky thought, His Excellency slept in a bed with mattress from the first night of his imprisonment and did not have to sleep on the ground as did everybody else, including Houston.

I immediately opened the *escritoire* and His Excellency dictated first an order to Filisola and then two others.

Commemoration of the Victory

Located in The San Jacinto Museum of History, which is in the base of The San Jacinto Monument, this plaque contains the names of those who participated in the battle on the Texas side. The monument opened in 1939. Alfred C. Finn was its architect.

Suggestions for Further Reading

Castañeda, Carlos E., editor and translator. *The Mexican Side of the Texas Revolution [1836]*. Dallas: P. L. Turner Company, 1928; Salem, New Hampshire: Ayer Company Publishers, Inc., 1976; New York: Arno Press, 1976.

De la Peña, José Enrique. *With Santa Anna in Texas: A Personal Narrative of the Revolution*. Translated and edited by Carmen Perry with an introduction by Llerna Friend. College Station: Texas A&M University Press, 1975.

Fehrenbach, T[heodore] R[eed]. *Lone Star: A History of Texas and the Texans*. New York: Macmillan Publishing Co., Inc., 1968.

Hardin, Stephen L. *Texian Iliad: A Military History of the Texas Revolution, 1835-1836*. Austin: University of Texas Press, 1994.

McDonald, Archie P. *The Trail to San Jacinto*. Boston: American Press, 1982.

Pohl, James W. *The Battle of San Jacinto*. [Austin:] Texas State Historical Association, 1989.

Places to Visit

The San Jacinto Monument, 3800 Park Road 1836, La Porte, Texas 77571-9744.

Museum exhibits, film presentation, and research library. Special events on April 21.